Original title:

Green Thoughts in a Grey Room

Copyright © 2025 Creative Arts Management OÜ
All rights reserved.

Author: Sophia Kingsley
ISBN HARDBACK: 978-1-80581-807-6
ISBN PAPERBACK: 978-1-80581-334-7
ISBN EBOOK: 978-1-80581-807-6

Verdant Breaths in a Lifeless Chamber

In a room where the walls are a sad, dull hue,
A plant with a quirk has a view just for two.
It giggles and wiggles, bright leaves all a-shiver,
While dust bunnies circle like clouds, oh, deliver!

The chair's squeaking loudly, a comedy show,
As the curtains get tickled by breezes that flow.
The lamp's glowing loudly, with a bulb's silly chat,
Like it's just had a joke with the couch and the mat.

A cactus, quite smug, wears a crown made of dust,
And plants on the shelf seem to plot and to rust.
They whisper of parties, where moss will be king,
In a dance with the shadows, what joy will they bring!

A gnome stirs awake from a nap oh so grand,
To join in the laughter, a ridiculous band.
With sticks for guitars and beetles on drums,
They'll rock this grey space till the sunlight becomes!

A Palette of Wishes

In a room so drab and dreary,
I thought of hues, oh so cheery,
Why not a splash of wild lime?
Or a dance of orange and thyme?

The curtains longing for a bloom,
Wishing for light to fill the gloom,
A brush of joy, a touch of flair,
To paint the walls with moments rare.

Flora's Resilience in Dusty Corners

In the corner, a cactus stands tall,
With dreams of sunlight, it answers the call,
Dust motes swirl like confetti near,
Cheering the plant, it shows no fear.

A sprig of hope in a pot full of grime,
Strives for glory, a fight quite sublime,
It chuckles softly at all the neglect,
Sipping on sunshine with perfect respect.

Serene Hues in the Gloom

The walls may whisper their dull, grey tune,
But I jest with shadows beneath the moon,
Cracks in the paint admire a grin,
As I giggle and twirl, let the fun begin!

A canvas of laughter, vibrant and wild,
Where mischief lurks just like a child,
Colors that dance, then waltz out of sight,
Turning monotony into delight.

Life Sprouts in the Shade

In the dimmest light, life finds a way,
Fragile green leaves laugh, come what may,
Peeking through shadows, where sunlight's shy,
They hold a party, beneath the sky.

Moss in the cracks does a jig with the dust,
Finding its rhythm—oh, how it must!
With roots in the floor, a fanciful thread,
Binding together dreams that were wed.

The Quiet Unfurling of Color

In a room where the dreariness stays,
A cactus is peak of its praise,
It waves like a hand,
In its prickly grandstand.

A fern in a pot so shy,
Watch it wither, oh my!
Yet it stretches with glee,
"Just a leaf," it does plea.

The wallpaper chuckles and peeks,
Muffled laughs in the creaks,
Beneath every frown,
A polka dot gown.

A single flower dares stand,
In this neglected land,
It whispers "I'm bright,"
"Why not join in delight?"

Hues of Serenity in a Lonely Room

The walls paint tales of woe,
Muted echoes in tow,
But the lamp's funny glow,
Makes shadows dance slow.

Cushions fluff in a line,
Like soldiers on wine,
Their colors may clash,
But they giggle and dash.

A plant in the corner sighs,
Wishing for less grey skies,
It dreams of a party,
Festooned and quite hearty.

The sofa shakes with mirth,
When jokes land on its girth,
In a world far too bleak,
They're the funnier streaks.

The Sunlight's Kiss on Forgotten Corners

Oh, the sunlight it glows,
Tickles the dust, then it goes,
While corners keep secrets,
In dust bunnies' retreats.

The shelf is a stage for dust,
Where the sunlight's a must,
It struts in like a star,
Though furniture's bizarre.

Mismatched socks play at hide,
In the cupboard where they reside,
A game of peek and flash,
"Find me, I'm not trash!"

The room boasts a smile wide,
Even with clutter inside,
Laughter's a blossom,
Where dreariness isn't the problem.

Flora's Whisper Through the Dust

A geranium hums a tune,
Under the flickering moon,
Its petals all wiggle,
As if sharing a giggle.

With scraggly weeds at their feet,
They plot every little greet,
"Dust, oh do stay away,
It's our party today!"

In this room quite absurd,
Nature whispers unheard,
While curtains conspire,
With dandelion attire.

A bamboo stick sways with flair,
While chairs play musical air,
In the merriest rebound,
Joy's laughter is found.

Vibrant Visions Beyond the Haze

In a room so grey and drear,
I daydream of a vibrant sphere.
A parrot dances on the floor,
While flower hats are all in store.

I painted clouds with lemon zest,
And made my couch a comfy nest.
The walls now laugh, they shimmy too,
As disco balls hang from the blue.

A cactus wearing shades, so bold,
Tells secrets that are yet untold.
I sip my tea with marshmallows,
While rabbits tango with the bellows.

So while the world is washed in grey,
I find my joy in every spray.
With every laugh, the colors bloom,
In this bizarre, delightful room.

The Color of Longing

In shadows deep where silence lingers,
I look for joy with silly fingers.
A rubber chicken on the chair,
Reminds me life must have some flair.

The curtains flutter, like a dance,
As I consider taking a chance.
A rainbow wand, I wave it high,
To paint my dreams across the sky.

The floor is a canvas—wild and neat,
I gently step with clumsy feet.
A glimpse of yellow through the gloom,
Transforms my heart, brightens the room.

I raise a toast with soda pop,
To colors that refuse to stop.
In longing's grip, I find my fun,
The grey retreats; the colors run.

Ferns and Fading Light

Ferns grow wild in corners dark,
While shadows dance, they leave a mark.
A disco ball has found its way,
To brighten up this dull cafe.

I make the sunlight wear a hat,
And give the cat a feathered spat.
On paper plates, my dreams are served,
With mint and laughter—oh, preserved!

The teapot sings a sassy tune,
As twilight sneaks in like a cartoon.
I giggle as the stars take flight,
Creating giggles in fading light.

In this strange room, a joy parade,
Where every color's unafraid.
With ferns and laughter taking turns,
In silly tales, my spirit yearns.

Where Hope Meets Obscurity

In a corner wrapped in mystery,
Hope prances 'round quite playfully.
A squirrel in a top hat pries,
At dreams that wander with surprise.

I paint the walls with jigsaw tunes,
And greet each day with dancing spoons.
A mystery novel, upside down,
Turns this grey frown into a crown.

The clock is melting, oh dear me!
It tells the time quite humorously.
With giggles tucked behind my ear,
I chase the shadows, void of fear.

Where hope and oddity collide,
In all the quirks, my heart can glide.
This room of grey is not so stark,
With laughter lighting up the dark.

Where Shadows Forget to Fall

A cactus in a hat, so bold,
Likes to dance when nights are cold.
The shadows giggle, what a sight!
As plants hold parties, with delight.

A fern sings songs of silly dreams,
While spiders weave their playful schemes.
A gnome is juggling, to and fro,
Who knew that moss could steal the show?

The walls are gray, but laughter blooms,
In every crevice, chaos looms.
With every chuckle, gloom takes flight,
While daisies clap in sheer delight.

So here we gather, side by side,
In this odd room where fun can't hide.
Forget your worries, let them stall,
In a space where shadows forget to fall.

Threads of Nature's Innovation.

Leaves are knitting scarves with flair,
Each stitch a tickle, in crisp air.
A squirrel spins tales of delight,
While acorns giggle at the sight.

The grass whispers secrets to the breeze,
Tiny insects hold meetings with ease.
A worm is teaching yoga right,
While daisies sport their crowns so bright.

In this wild room of vibrant cheer,
Nature plots laughter, far and near.
With every twist, and every twirl,
It's a spicy concoction, give it a whirl.

Forget the gray, bring forth the jest,
In the heart of chaos, we are blessed.
Threads of laughter weaves so tight,
In a room where all things come to light.

Whispers of Verdant Dreams

In a corner, the ivy sings,
Of wild adventures and crazy flings.
Lettuce giggles, hops on a chair,
While turnips gossip without a care.

The broccoli brings a joke to share,
"Why did the pepper hide? It's bare!"
Tomatoes chuckle, blushing red,
As herbs declare they're mischief led.

The walls might frown in dull grey hue,
But nature winks, it knows what's true.
With every laugh that takes its flight,
The bloom of joy is pure delight.

So let us dance in this quaint room,
With whispers bright, to chase the gloom.
In verdant daydreams, we shall stay,
As laughter leads us on our way.

Shadows Over Emerald Echoes

Amidst the gloom, a plant does sway,
Tickling shadows that come to play.
The petunias plot a funny dance,
While moonlight winks at fate's romance.

The curtains rustle, gossiping leaves,
With stories that no one truly believes.
A fuchsia sprout plays peek-a-boo,
As nightfall brings the laughter anew.

In this grey room, a carnival thrives,
Where plants behave like bonafide jives.
With echoes of emerald joy about,
It's a riotous gathering, without a doubt.

So join the party, let shadows blend,
With mirthful moments around each bend.
For here in this odd little space,
Laughter and life find their perfect place.

Cracks in the Concrete

In the cracks of the sidewalk, a sprout jumps high,
Poking through stones, it winks at the sky.
"Hello world!" it shouts with glee,
While pigeons just stare, "Who let you be?"

A dandelion giggles, a flower with flair,
"I'm just a weed, don't you dare compare!"
In the midst of the gray, it dances so bold,
Wearing sunshine as armor, never to fold.

Life Emerges

In a dusty old pot, forgotten and bare,
A cactus sneezes, shedding its despair.
"A little water?" It looks quite divine,
But its only companion is a bottle of wine.

A fern finds a crevice, a party it trails,
"Who knew I'd grow here?" It flaunts as it hails.
Laughter erupts from this botanical crew,
In a quiet little room where only they grew.

Vibrant Thoughts Amongst the Ashes

Amongst the burnt toast, a green sprout does twirl,
With a wink and a nudge, it laughs as it unfurls.
"Is this breakfast? Or some kind of joke?"
A whispering chive teases, ready to poke.

A petunia prances on a smoke-dusted ledge,
"I'm a bloom in disguise, at the edge of the hedge!"
The charcoal just chuckles, embracing the plight,
As the kitchen remains a chaotic delight.

The Heartbeat of Green in Stillness

A cactus in silence, with dreams in its spines,
Practices yoga, finds its own lines.
"Breathe in the stillness!" It hums with great zest,
While the houseplant rolls eyes, longing for jest.

In a pot full of snores, a basil takes stage,
Declaring, "I'm fresh! I'm all the rage!"
As the dust bunnies cheer from a shadowy room,
With a pinch of humor, they challenge the gloom.

Serene Ferns in Whispered Corners

In corners of silence, a fern starts to giggle,
Tickled by shadows, it can barely wiggle.
"I'm the life of the party!" it chirps with delight,
While the dust settles softly, seeking its night.

A spider spins webs, counting each sprout,
Whispering secrets, what life's all about.
Through beams of sunlight, they plot their grand show,
In a room full of echoes, they'll steal the whole glow.

A Garden of Dreams in Dullness

In corners where dust bunnies hop,
A cactus dreams of a wild crop.
Imagining jungles in potbound sighs,
While the sun never peeks, but a lamp tries.

The daisies roll their eyes at the floor,
Moss chuckles at the open drawer.
They giggle at socks, mismatched and bright,
Wishing for rain, but it's just a slight blight.

The spider spins tales of a funky dance,
As books collect dust, they miss the chance.
To sprout in the corners, break free of the gloom,
Instead, they're stuck in this room with no bloom.

Yet there's humor in wilted green frills,
As laughter blooms with the first spring chills.
In dullness, they find their silliness sweet,
Crafting a garden that can't be beat.

Life's Palette in a Darkened Space

A splash of sunlight under a chair,
Pats the shadows, much like a dare.
Bright colors whisper beneath the grey,
As crayons sigh on a damp paper tray.

Paint cans dream of a wild free spree,
While brushes ponder a life by the sea.
But here they sit, with hopes on a shelf,
Like forgotten dishes, they gather their self.

A polka dot mug, chipped and eccentric,
Mocks the grey walls, that's just so pedestrian.
It holds a secret, a brew of delight,
Wishing for moments both messy and bright.

So, let's dance like the stains on the wall,
Each splatter tells stories both silly and small.
In this dim-lit space, a riot of cheer,
Life's palette shimmies, it's almost here!

The Grit of Leaves in Urban Gloom

Amidst the concrete, some leaves peek through,
Whispering secrets like they always do.
A skateboard flies, just misses a root,
While pigeons mock on a nearby commute.

The weeds strut proudly, wearing their crowns,
In cracked pavements, they snag silly frowns.
They giggle in wind, toss their little bets,
On which side of the sidewalk will gather respect.

Vines laugh at fences, doing their best,
To climb all the way to the roof of the nest.
Their antics entwined in a dizzying race,
As city folk hurry, they just save face.

A splash of color, a bold, cheeky leaf,
Turns frowns to grins, brings moments of grief.
In urban gloom, where laughter is rare,
The grit of nature is still everywhere!

Petals Drifting on a Grey Breeze

A petal drifts lightly, with dreams in tow,
Sailing through silence, sneakily slow.
It catches a giggle from red cheeked blooms,
And whispers the laughter that always resumes.

On grey breezes, it twirls with delight,
Daring the clouds to join in the flight.
But oh, how they pout, with damp little frowns,
While the petal just laughs, stealing the crowns.

A dandelion's wish floats up to the sky,
"I'll conquer the gloom, come with me, oh my!"
With a puff, it starts tickling heads all around,
As flowers rejoice—who knew fun could be found?

So dance, little petal, on whims of the air,
Through all of the gray, spread laughter and care.
In moments of drab, let joy intercede,
For petals and laughter are all that we need.

Echoes of Renewal in a Silent Haven

In corners where dust bunnies thrive,
A cactus dances, feeling alive.
The sofa, though frayed, wears a smile,
Wishing for guests to stay for a while.

The clock ticks on, a slow-motion show,
While plants send whispers, 'Hey, look at me grow!'
And shadows play tag on the wall, what a sight,
In this cozy chaos, everything feels right.

A nothing-y space becomes quite the scene,
With rubber plants plotting to overthrow clean.
Each pot holds a secret, a story to tell,
About mischief and laughter, oh do stay awhile.

So here's to the laughter in every nook,
In a room filled with green things, come take a look.
Where renewal and glee swirl in delightful refrain,
Echoes of joy in this cluttered domain.

Lush Memories Amongst Shadows

Underneath the dusty old desk,
A rubber tree dreams of a dance so grotesque.
Old socks hanging out in a comical twist,
Reciting the tales that no one would miss.

A fern winks slyly, as if to say,
'Who needs sunshine? I've got this room gray!'
The rug hums a tune of lost socks and glee,
While an antique lamp nods along with the spree.

Moldy old pizza? A treasure, not fate!
Nature insists we just recreate.
With every spilled drink, and errant cheer,
Lush memories blossom in shadows, oh dear!

So let laughter tumble amidst the old gloom,
As friends gather round in this enchanted room.
In the furrows of chaos, joy we'll extract,
In lush, funny moments, soft warmth we'll enact.

Fragments of Nature in Urban Silence

Between the routers and tangled cords,
A forgotten plant, a warrior of hoards.
It shimmies each time the fridge opens wide,
Bringing fresh air where the silence might hide.

A pot full of dirt with a sprout that's a tease,
It sways to the rhythm of passing cars' wheeze.
And the window, oh the window, cracked just enough,
Invites silly breezes, none of them tough.

A tiny cactus in a coffee mug,
It dreams of the desert, snug and a hug.
Dust motes like fairies dance in the light,
While inside a pot, a riot takes flight.

In urban depths where silence whispers,
Nature brings laughter, with all of its twisters.
Fragments unite in a fun little dance,
In this quirky haven, give humor a chance.

Blossoms Amidst Grey Walls

Amidst the harsh walls of monotone hue,
A single daisy declares, 'I made it through!'
It's winking at shadows, saying, 'Cheer up, dude!'
Where laughter lurks quiet, nature's the mood.

The curtains are drapes of a long-gone style,
Yet vines twist and tangle, oh, what a smile!
They creep along edges and seem to recite,
Stories of joy in the still of the night.

Old furniture speaks of a time full of cheer,
When cushions had flair and no vacuum near.
Yet here we find magic in petals that flare,
Where blooms burst forth, sweet aromas to share.

With every odd corner and sentiment grand,
Walls hear the laughter that nature had planned.
Amongst grey and weary, let colors emerge,
In this funny retreat, let the blossoms surge.

Cracks of Color in a Monochrome World

In a room that's all dull and grey,
A gnome with a tie leads the way.
He paints with such flair,
While birds watch in despair.

A cactus does dance on the shelf,
Sipping tea, quite proud of itself.
The curtains yell loud,
'We want fun, not a cloud!'

The walls whisper tales of delight,
Of parties that spark every night.
Yet here we just piddle,
With plants and their fiddle.

Still, the laughter just might ignite,
A riot of colors, so bright!
Let's swap out this gloom,
And invite in the bloom!

Fragments of Nature's Breath

In corners where shadows all sprawl,
A lizard recites Shakespeare for all.
His accent is grand,
Yet no one can stand.

A flower peeks out from the floor,
Singing ballads oh-so-chore.
With petals that sway,
It begs folks to play.

There's grass growing high on the chair,
Moss tickles toes, it's a dare!
While dust bunnies cheer,
'The party is here!'

Oh, let's plant some seeds in this sight,
And make this dull room feel just right.
With a giggle, a wink,
We'll turn grey into ink!

The Scent of Spring in a Dim Space

A smell of fresh blooms fills the air,
But it's just the old socks, I swear!
A bee in a hat,
Cheers, 'Ain't this a spat?'

The dust bunnies do a jig on the floor,
While mice debate Shakespearean lore.
With a flick of the tail,
They script out a tale.

The sun peeks in with a wink,
But curtains hold tight, what a blink!
A plant in the pot,
Simply laughing a lot.

In this room of passed time and tales,
Where laughter rolls in like soft gales.
Let's dance to the cheer,
And toast to the weird!

Radiance Amidst the Drab

In this room of muted gloom,
A goldfish is plotting to zoom.
With fins made of spark,
He's aiming for a lark.

The old clock ticks slow, such a snore,
As mushrooms debate their next score.
They plan quite a feast,
With humor, at least!

A chair takes a stand, claims it's art,
While pillows make jokes, play their part.
Together they sway,
In a strange little ballet.

Oh, let's splash some paint on these walls,
With giggles and grace, let's have balls!
For laughter can grow,
In the dim, let it glow!

Flickers of Growth in Greyed Enclosures

In a pot that sits with dust,
A tiny sprout dares to trust.
'Who knew I could be so bold?'
While the walls whisper tales of old.

With each small leaf, a laugh ensues,
Tickling gloom with rebellious hues.
'I'm not just a weed in disguise,'
Shouts the sprout, aiming for the skies.

Shadows chuckle, 'You're quite absurd!'
'Oh please,' it grins, 'I'm quite the bird!'
In secret corners, wildlings play,
As sunlight fights to find a way.

Chasing dreams in earthen beds,
Where concrete jokes just scratch their heads.
Flashing colors, with all their might,
In the grey, they dance, what a sight!

Traces of Life Searching for Light

In a corner where all seems still,
A hint of green brings forth a thrill.
'Excuse me, could you be so bright?'
The shadows nod, a humorous sight.

Roots tap dance beneath the floor,
While dust bunnies cheer and roar.
Leaving trails of laughter wide,
As life continues, trying to hide.

Walls creak out a funny tune,
As seedlings stretch, beneath the moon.
'You think you've got this space to claim?'
They giggle softly, 'We're not the same!'

In this room where shadows loom,
Tiny greens burst forth, there's plenty of room.
With every giggle, a leaf unfurls,
As life reveals its whacky pearls.

Whimsical Greens in a Gloomy Setting

In a drab old box, once unadorned,
A sprightly green has now been born.
It flutters just to tease the grey,
While chuckling softly, 'I'm here to stay!'

Though the sun plays hide and seek,
This little leaf feels quite unique.
'What's a little gloom to me?'
It winks and sways, full of glee.

Casting shadows in playful forms,
It whispers jokes to all the norms.
'Look at me, in this gloomy place!'
With each bright wave, it shares the grace.

Textures dance in the dull space,
While laughter blooms with dainty grace.
In this quiet spot, life has flair,
Colors giggle, banishing despair.

The Beauty of Contrast in Stillness

In a room where silence reigns,
A cactus strikes up silly claims.
'I may be prickly, but just look!'
It grins wide, stealing the book.

Next to it, a pot of thyme,
Exclaims, 'I'm here to make a rhyme!'
With every leaf, it shakes its head,
'We'll have a party, hop out of bed!'

Gloomy walls can't hold us back,
We're the punchline in grey's track.
'Let's dance!' they shout, bold and spry,
For laughter blooms, and grey slips by.

As both unite in soft delight,
They ponder jokes on long, dark nights.
The beauty shines in stark contrast,
In stillness, joy could never last.

Pulse of Nature in a Silent Room

In a room so dull, I saw a tree,
It waved a branch, said, "Look at me!"
The air grew thick with a fragrant joke,
As a cactus giggled, and a fern bespoke.

The chair turned green with envy bright,
While the lampshade sighed with all its might.
An idle pot got jealous too,
Broke a leg, cried, "I won't grow for you!"

Toothbrushes danced on the plastic floor,
While socks debated the meaning of four.
The walls looked on in potted glee,
As the clock hummed a tune of harmony.

Oh, nature's pulse in boredom's throat,
Grows laughter loud in a rubber boat.
In silence, there's whimsy, so brace yourself,
For joy blooms best atop a dusty shelf.

Engraved in Lushness

On the wall, vines carved a witty quip,
Boys could learn from this fine grip.
A spider spun tales of trampoline swings,
While grumpy old soil complained of things.

Cucumbers giggled under their weight,
Applauding the salad that sealed their fate.
'It's not a joke!' the lettuce cried,
As it rolled off the counter, a leaf untried.

In this room where the couch plushily laid,
The curtains whispered secrets well-played.
An avocado peeked, soft as can be,
While the fridge hummed, "You can't catch me!"

Inscribed in this green, a mischief song,
Where fingers of nature apparently belong.
Engraving laughter, as pots flip their lids,
May your life be a salad, not a series of bids!

Bound in Shadows

In corners deep where plants conspire,
They chuckle low, like a leafy choir.
A shadow stretched with a grumpy frown,
Weighed down by love for the old grey town.

"Whatcha doing, shadow?" a petunia teased,
"Writing a memoir of being displeased?"
It quipped back softly with a wink of a leaf,
"Don't bother me, I'm gathering grief!"

The carpet sighed, all fibers in knots,
As socks held meetings on ins and outs.
In the dark, even dust has a voice,
Making metaphors amidst the noise.

Bound in shadows, a tale to unfold,
Every snicker and whisper, a memory told.
Even in gloom, humor finds a way,
As laughter emerges, brightening the day.

The Soft Echo of Forgotten Gardens

Once a garden, now a room,
With echoes of laughter chasing doom.
A rose reminisced of a tight embrace,
While daisies juggled with charming grace.

Reclining petals said, "What a mess!"
As plums and apricots played poker in dress.
Through the window, the wind gave a laugh,
While ginger roots crafted a marvelous path.

The marble floors, oh, they snickered sweet,
While snails debated the best way to eat.
Every seed remembers the sun's warm kiss,
Creating a ruckus in joyful bliss.

Echoing soft, the whispers of yore,
Dancing with laughter, the roots implore.
Join in the fun of a forgotten place,
Where gardens and giggles leave no trace.

Verdancy in a Sea of Ash

In piles of grey, a sprout dared to grow,
It cracked a smile, putting on a show.
"Hey there, ash!" it called with glee,
"Can't you see you're not scaring me?"

The dust bunnies laughed, wheezing with cheer,
"We've hosted more parties, come join us here!"
While twigs formed a band in rooty delight,
Playing tunes to dance under dead night.

A lonely light bulb flickered its way,
Shining bright like it just won the day.
"Bring out the salad!" a potato did shout,
"In this world of ash, we're all that's about!"

So, verdancy laughed in the darkest of rooms,
Dancing with zest through the ashy glooms.
For life finds a way, a humorous twist,
In a world of grey, laugh—you'll persist!

When Greens Whisper to Grays

In a room where shadows play,

The plants have secrets, come what may.
They chuckle low, beneath the dust,
And discuss how rust is simply mistrust.

The drab walls listen with faux surprise,
While leafy friends share their leafy ties.
"Why so serious?" a fern might jest,
As the paint chips fall, feeling quite blessed.

A cactus winks with spiny flair,
"Life's too short; give laughter air!"
Between the gloom and chaos dance,
The whispers bloom into a trance.

In the corner, a plant pot grins,
While drizzles of color are where fun begins.
Laughter reels through every crevice,
Taking the gray out with pure levity bliss.

Vignettes of Life on an Unpainted Canvas

A canvas bare with blurry sights,

Pigeons prance in mismatched tights.
They paint their lives in hues of cheer,
While dust bunnies roll on without fear.

The brushes giggle against the void,
In messiness, creativity's buoyed.
A paint splatter's a playful swish,
As they fight for space—a colorful wish.

The papers rustle, joining in jest,
"No brush can capture a whimsy fest!"
With laughter drawn in crooked lines,
They map out joys through pastels and signs.

Life unframed in quirky ways,
In this room, imagination stays.
Each unmade stroke breaks the calm,
Bringing laughter's soothing balm.

Touch of Vibrance in the Stillness

A stillness lingers, heavy and bold,

Yet below the surface, stories unfold.
A radiator coughs a rusty tune,
While curtains sway as if to swoon.

The dust motes dance, audaciously spry,
"Come one, come all! We don't even try!"
A bright sock dangles in the gloom,
Forever lost, yet bursting with bloom.

A shadow mocks a comical plight,
As the clock grumbles, wishing for night,
But each tick laughs with its own delay,
In this quiet, there's always play.

The sill creaks in gleeful glee,
Inviting whimsy, it's plain to see.
In brief moments, the colors collide,
Turning stillness into a joyride.

Tales of Renewal in a Lifeless Chamber

In a chamber dull and void of dreams,

Hope tiptoes softly on rickety beams.
A dust-covered chair cracks a bad pun,
"Why don't we finish? We're nowhere, hon!"

The wallpaper peels like an aging joke,
While laughter erupts from a forgotten cloak.
"What if renewal involves a wild dance?"
A spirit clouds twirl, caught in a trance.

An old lamp flickers, feeling so bright,
"Let's jazz it up! We're alive tonight!"
With every flicker, they find their groove,
And the shadows shimmy, trying to move.

Excitement brews in the stale air,
As laughter bubbles, abundant and rare.
In lifeless corners, reawakening glows,
With tales told anew, as the laughter flows.

Echoing Life Beneath Everyday Chaos

In the clutter, a cactus grins,
A rubber plant doing gym spins.
Papers fly like wild little birds,
While I'm just trying to find my words.

The desk is a jungle, oh what a sight,
With pens as vines, all tangled tight.
A mouse scurries, I'm sure it's a spy,
An office safari where deadlines lie.

Ferns Flourishing in the Quietude

Ferns wave hello, lush and bright,
In shadows where I can't find the light.
They chat with dust bunnies, oh so sly,
I swear they plot while I just sigh.

A peace lily winks with a cheeky grin,
Rooted in humor, my daily win.
They gossip as I sip on my tea,
Plant life banter—just let it be free!

Silhouettes of Hope Against Somber Walls

In the dim where laughter hides,
Are shadows of joy, bright future strides.
Post-it notes, a colorful crew,
Chasing away the grey like a shoe.

A weed pops up, bold and spry,
In the cracks of my mundane sky.
Each crumpled corner offers a laugh,
Life's quirky math, a sweet craft.

A Glimpse of Eden through Dusty Windows

Through smudged panes, the sun peeks in,
A sparkle of life where shadows spin.
Dust motes dance like tiny fairies,
While I'm stuck here with my worries slow and scary.

A tangle of ivy climbs on high,
Whispering secrets to passersby.
Oh, the stories wrapped in green spice,
Make even the grey seem rather nice!

The Resurgence of Life in Dark Corners

Dust bunnies dance with glee,
While cockroaches throw a spree.
In the shadow of the chair,
A fuzzball dreams without a care.

Moss grows thick on the forgotten shoe,
Whispering tales of what once flew.
A spider spins a silver thread,
Crafting stories in silence, instead.

Old toys scheme in musty gloom,
Planning pranks to chase the doom.
A paperclip forms a tiny crew,
To venture where no one's got a clue.

In the corners, laughter roams,
Painting joy on dusty domes.
Who knew chaos could also bloom,
In such a comically grey room?

Sprouts of Inspiration in Silent Walls

Pictures of squirrels hang on the frame,
While daydreams play a silly game.
Cracks in the wall hum low tunes,
To the beat of forgotten cartoons.

A potted plant sings a lullaby,
While coffee cups wink slyly, oh my!
Post-its gossip about the day,
Jokes told in a pastel ballet.

There's a joke book wedged in between,
Where laughter echoes, sweet and obscene.
The calendar rolls in fits of glee,
Celebrating moments mostly unseen.

Under the wallpaper, secrets crawl,
Roaming the tales plastered on the wall.
In this quiet realm of whimsical charm,
Joy sprouts where it feels disarmed.

Hiding Gemstones Amongst the Grit

Adventurous crumbs plot their next feast,
In a kingdom ruled by a mischievous beast.
A rubber band slingshot's a royal decree,
For all to engage in delightful spree.

Crumbs are treasures, scattered with flair,
While the fridge hums a tune with care.
Nail clippings challenge the spatula's might,
In a playful duel that lasts through the night.

Lost socks are pirates on a bold quest,
Searching for their mates, never to rest.
In the abyss, a lollipop hides,
With whispers of sweet and sticky tides.

Cups catch the light with glittery gleam,
Reflecting the laughter from a dream.
In this space where mischief is lit,
Cherished gems hide in nooks, bit by bit.

Memory of Sunlight in a Clouded Room

Curtains dance in a flickering light,
As dust mites hold a disco night.
In the dim, a laughter floats,
From the moths who wear fancy coats.

A forgotten chair plays peek-a-boo,
Imagining sunshine, a warm brew.
Phantom rays poke through the grey,
Mischief mingling in a playful sway.

The clock ticks on with a sleepy grin,
While shadows plot a whimsical spin.
Whispers of sunshine in the air,
Giggling snacks from the pantry dare.

Memory wraps its arms, snug and tight,
In a room where joy meets gloom, just right.
Every corner glows with a silly beam,
Crafting laughter from a faded dream.

Nature's Resilience in an Urban Nook

In a tiny pot, a plant survives,
Peeking out to see city drives.
A brave little sprout with dreams so wide,
Dodging pigeons while trying to hide.

Amidst the clamor of honking cars,
It whispers secrets to passing stars.
"Why fuss with traffic? Just look at me!"
A dandelion laughs, "I'm wild and free!"

An alley cat stops to give a glare,
While daffodils dance in the cool night air.
Concrete will frown, but petals won't care,
For a touch of color is all that's fair.

Verdant Light Amidst the Shadows

Sunlight splatters on walls so grey,
Cacti in pots cheerfully sway.
A broccoli tree in the kitchen nook,
"Eat your veggies!" it gives a look.

In the dusty corner, a fern snores loud,
Dreaming of jungles, feeling quite proud.
"I'm subtropical!" it whispers low,
While the slippers get jealous, feeling so slow.

Lettuce in salad begins to squawk,
"A witty remark!" says the wise old rock.
Nature debates with echoes of man,
Who knew greenery had such a plan?

The Glow of Green in a Gloomy Realm

Moss in the corner gives a sly wink,
As if to say, "Come, have a drink!"
With glimmers of hope hidden from sight,
Inviting all to join in the plight.

The cactus chuckles, "I'm spiky but sweet,
Try giving me water; it's quite a treat!"
While lilies giggle by a gloomy lamp,
They strategize ways to plant a happy stamp.

A rogue little fungus begins to dance,
Joining the party, a merry romance.
In a world so dull, there's humor unfurled,
As the green revelers take on the world!

Petals vs. Concrete: A Standoff

Petals are pouting, facing the street,
Concrete is boasting, feeling elite.
"Shake your branches!" the roses demand,
Can't we agree? Let's make a stand!

Without watering can, the petals took bets,
"Who'll hold out longer?" a sunflower frets.
Concrete just chuckles, unmoved by the fuss,
"I've got tall buildings! Who needs a blush?"

Came a storm cloud with wiggly rain,
"Oh, please! Not me!" cried a daisy in vain.
Yet, with each drop came a jubilant cheer,
Buds started blooming—oh, what a year!

The Echo of Bloom within Shadows

In corners where the dust bunnies play,
A cactus whispers jokes to the sway.
The geraniums giggle, quite snug in their pots,
While violets tell secrets we all have forgot.

A rubber plant's tale of a lost shoe,
Brings laughter and joy, like morning dew.
The ferns reminisce of a party once wild,
With ivy dancing 'round like a playful child.

Sunbeams land softly, like feathers afloat,
As the shadows all chuckle, they connect every note.
Even the air has a twist of delight,
In this room where gray meets the colors so bright.

A squirrel bursts in, with a nut in his cheek,
He winks at the daisies, it's comedy peak.
Who knew that a bloom in a shadowy space,
Could brighten a heart with such memorable grace?

Luminescence in a Veiled Room

In a nook where the light dares to play,
Chives and thyme have something to say.
Their whispers of flavor fill up the air,
While curtains of gray just stand there and stare.

With each little sprout comes a tickle and tease,
The shadows all giggle, take life with such ease.
Old books in the corner, they've heard every rhyme,
As the fungus on the floor begins to chime.

A lamp flickers on, casting shapes like a clown,
Cornflowers blush deep as they tumble down.
The potted basil dreams of grand gourmet,
While rosemary rolls her eyes at decay.

The ceiling may frown with its paint chipped and sore,
But laughter will linger and dance on the floor.
In this veiled room, with its bright little spark,
A party spins on, igniting the dark.

Nature's Pulse in a Still Chamber

In the stillness, a tickle creeps by,
Nasturtiums chuckle, beneath the white sky.
A pot-bellied plant plays a game of charades,
While air freshener laughs, in a scent-filled charade.

A rubbery leaf becomes quite the star,
As it tells stories of adventures afar.
The soil drives the roots to jump up and sing,
In this undisturbed room, oh, what joy they bring!

A cactus is plotting a new kind of dance,
While a dandelion dreams of a wild romanced chance.
The shadows play tag, in their ghostly attire,
Like a stand-up routine at a lounge by the fire.

And though this place seems so dull and so bland,
Nature's odd humor brings life to the stand.
In a chamber so silent, the laughs do resound,
As the heartbeat of green spins joy all around.

A Symphony of Color in Monochrome

In black and white, the plants take a bow,
Mimicking laughter at the stiff curtain's vow.
Chlorophyll dreams, tittering in the shade,
Challenging grey with every slick move made.

A thistle in bloom, quite the comedian here,
Telling tales of travels, bringing giggles and cheer.
Fern fronds toss in rhythm, like swings in a park,
While monochrome walls turn bright with each spark.

Tiny ants march in their suits of fine line,
Debating the pigment, "Is black really divine?"
The shadows blend in, creating a scene,
Where patterns of humor, they craft and they glean.

So let's toast the flora that glow in the grey,
With chuckles and tales to brighten the day.
For in every dull chamber, there's humor to bloom,
A symphony plays in this monochrome room.

Solitude of Nature's Palette

In a corner, the cactus sings,
With neighbors who chip off their wings.
The daisies giggle in quiet tones,
While toadstools plan parties of scones.

A tree in the corner shares a joke,
While the moss rolls its eyes, the old bloke.
A snail slides by, slick and slow,
Whispering secrets only worms know.

The paint on the walls starts to peel,
Laughing at dreams in its concealed feel.
A fern does a dance, all wobbly and spry,
While the shadows just watch, with a sigh.

In this vibrant soft haze, more silly than smart,
Even the silence plays a funny part.
For when joy is painted all over the gloom,
Life turns a room into nature's own bloom.

Reflections in a Dim Garden

A shadow rabbit hops with flair,
Wearing wildflowers, yet none to spare.
The gnomes are debating who's funnier
As the sun dips down, stirring the blurry.

A crow caws riddles by the old gate,
While the lilies nod, declaring fate.
The hedges conspire, whisper and snicker,
As night falls, their gossip grows thicker.

The moon arrives, all dressed in white,
Tickling the petals gently at night.
"Why does the grass always seem so neat?"
Perhaps it just wanted a cozy seat.

In this dim retreat, where the laughter blooms,
A garden of giggles ignites the rooms.
For in every shadow, there's always a glint,
A spark of joy where the shy spirits hint.

Hues of Hope Under Gloom

Under grey skies, the daisies shout,
With petals so bright, they giggle about.
A parade of leaves dances along,
While clouds grumble low, singing their song.

The raindrops chuckle, what a sight!
Turning puddles into sheer delight.
A snail races by on borrowed time,
Yelling, "Slow and steady, I can still rhyme!"

In corners, the shadows do a jig,
As sunlight pokes in, rather big.
Each blade of grass tells its own tale,
Of rain dances and breezes that sail.

So let gloom dissolve in this playful brigade,
As nature paints bright in a joyful parade.
For under the grey, there's laughter and cheer,
In every heartbeat, a song we can hear.

The Sprout Beneath the Surface

Beneath the soil, a sprout stretched wide,
Dreaming of sunshine and a great green ride.
It giggles with worms, all wiggly and spry,
While saying to rocks, "Can I give it a try?"

The beetles roll dice, sharing their fate,
As roots whisper secrets, none hesitate.
"Who needs the sun when you're underground?
A kingdom of soil, where laughter is found!"

A shy little flower peeks out for a glance,
"Who knew that dirt could hold such a dance?"
With ants as their band, playing quick tunes,
While the shadows above conspire and swoon.

So let there be joy, even down deep,
Where dreams sprout fun, and secrets do leap.
For hidden in gloom, there's always a jest,
Nature's own humor is truly the best!

Chasing Light in a Cloistered Space

In a corner where shadows play,
A sunbeam skids through the fray.
Chasing dust bunnies on the wall,
Light giggles, weaves, and does a sprawl.

A plant in a pot looks quite prim,
Sips water by the edge of whim.
It rolls its leaves in a playful dance,
While I just sit, lost in a trance.

The ceiling sighs, the floor has creaks,
Yet silence here is full of peaks.
A daydream blooms, spills over its edges,
I'm giggling at my own life's ledges.

A haphazard sky under a roof,
Rain and sun both have their proof.
In this nook, laughter takes its flight,
Chasing whims in a cloistered light.

The Gravity of Growth in Stagnation

In my room, the wallpaper peels,
But my dreams spin like soup on wheels.
A cactus claims the windowsill,
Waving its arms with an everlasting thrill.

The chair rumbles, I swear it sighs,
It's tired of housing all my lies.
Yet, I'm stuck here, quite the sight,
Orbits collide in a clueless flight.

Mismatched socks dance on the floor,
Who knew laundry could cause such uproar?
Gravity pulls, but I refuse to fall,
My head's in the clouds—who needs it all?

With every whim and gossip of leaves,
I ponder my chances, or playful thieves.
Growing roots in this stagnant space,
Laughing at nowhere—oh, what a race!

Heartbeats of Nature's Refuge

A fern sits solemn, and it knows,
The pulse beneath all the woes.
With every tick and tock of time,
It sneezes green—come, share the rhyme!

A squirrel can't find his acorns lost,
He rages on, but what a cost!
Yet outside my prison, nature hums,
While in here, I've lost my thumbs.

The air is thick with all things stale,
Yet a ladybug arrives with flair.
She shakes her tiny head at me,
"Come outdoors, you'll fit with glee!"

Heartbeats echo through stillness thick,
Nature whispers with a flick.
I laugh aloud at my own sad cage,
Finding peace in this silent stage.

Colors Breaching the Abyss of Dullness

In the carpet, a lonely flower fades,
Complaining 'bout life in monochrome shades.
With a laugh, I ask it to perk,
But it just grumbles—ah, the work!

The walls are beige, as bland as can be,
Yet dreams explode in boisterous spree.
A crayon box spills from my drawer,
Colors clash on the polished floor.

The clock chimes a most dreadful song,
But paintbrushes dance—it won't be long.
I swirl in hues, I riot in cheer,
Who knew dullness had so much fear?

Those colors jump, disobey the rule,
Transforming plain into a vibrant school.
I thrive in chaos, oh what a view,
Dullness, you've met your colorful due!

Whispers of Verdant Dreams

In a room so dull and bland,
A cactus danced, a leafy band.
It swayed and jived, a comical sight,
While I chuckled, it took flight.

A fern wore shades, so cool and bright,
Pretending it was day, not night.
The windows sighed, the walls did groan,
'Let us join, you green alone!'

A pot of herbs was on a spree,
Spilling secrets to a lonely bee.
They plotted ways to paint the drab,
With bursts of color, oh what a gab!

So let this room be filled with cheer,
As nature's jesters bring good cheer.
In every crack, a laugh shall bloom,
As we share jokes in this grey room!

Echoes of Emerald Whimsy

In a space where shadows creep,
A parrot laughed while I lost sleep.
Just outside, a tree would tease,
'Come out and dance, at least, please!'

A flower pot donned a grin,
While home dust bunnies danced within.
"Get up!" said thyme, "it's time to play!"
"Before the sun just fades away!"

The lamp was jealous of the plants,
"It won't hurt to try a few pranks!"
So off they went, a leafy crew,
To paint the drab in bursting hue.

Alas, the sofa let out a sigh,
As ivy claimed the chair nearby.
In this room where laughter flows,
Nature's jesters steal the show!

Shadows of Nature's Muse

In corners dark and corners bare,
A potted palm began to care.
"Let's lift this drear with some delight,
A comedy show, we'll do it right!"

A dandelion, bold and brash,
Made jokes with every little flash.
"Let's sprout laughter! Come what may,
In this room, let joy hold sway!"

The curtains giggled at their plight,
"Join the fun, we're soft and light!"
So they'd sway, dance, twirl, and spin,
Nature's party would soon begin.

Underneath a greyish hue,
A riot of laughter, fresh and new.
In shadows deep, where doubts reside,
A green revolution starts to glide!

Lush Reveries in Concrete Walls

In concrete walls with cracks galore,
A jade vine peeked, said, "What's in store?"
With such a view, dreary and tame,
It challenged gloom to a funny game.

"Let's trick the light, make shadows play,
Invite the sun to join our fray!"
With every leaf, a giggle came,
The mundane bent, forgetting shame.

A rubber plant got bold and sly,
Offering seeds of laughter high.
"Come, let's dance upon this floor,
And make these walls a stage encore!"

With every petal, humor spread,
The humble room was joyfully fed.
And in the grey, they made their start,
A lush coronation of the heart!

Breaths of Wildness in an Urban Stronghold

In a city filled with concrete walls,
A squirrel races through the shopping malls.
With tiny sunglasses on its nose,
It struts like it owns the place, who knows?

Pigeons fashion hats from coffee cups,
While taxi drivers shout, "Hey, what's up?"
A jogger trips over a pizza slice,
As laughter echoes, it's so precise.

A dog in a bowtie chases its tail,
While office workers dream of a trail.
"Why not a beach?" one loudly proclaims,
"Instead of this city of trains and games?"

In this urban maze, we find our cheer,
Amidst the traffic, we hold life dear.
So let the city be our funny stage,
As we dance on the streets like a wild page.

Tints of Joy in a Muted Atmosphere

In a world of beige, a flower blooms bright,
Turning heads with its sheer delight.
A painter spills color, oh what a scene,
As smiles spread wide, quite unforeseen!

Coffee shops filled with laughter and cheer,
A croissant wears sprinkles, what a career!
The barista sings tunes while pouring your cup,
"Who needs a frown? Just sip it up!"

A cat in a hat struts down the lane,
While people look twice, a moment of gain.
Umbrellas join in a whimsical dance,
Turning dull walks into a joyous prance.

In muted corners, colors play hide and seek,
With giggles and chuckles, we hear them speak.
So let's paint our lives with laughter's hue,
In a canvas of smiles, where dreams come true.

The Dance of the Leaves in Solitude

In autumn's chill, a leaf takes flight,
Twisting and turning with sheer delight.
"I'm off to find friends," it calls with glee,
While crickets quietly hum their decree.

A tree wearing sweaters shakes in the breeze,
As squirrels debate about winter trees.
"Three nuts or two?" one whispers with pride,
While clouds chuckle, performing outside.

Fog rolls in like a ghostly mime,
As branches wave to the rhythm of time.
A lonely tummy grumbles, quite bold,
"Lunch break is here, I'm hungry for gold!"

Leaves join the dance, a spiraling spree,
As laughter wraps around the old oak tree.
In solitude, they create a party,
So come join the fun, don't be tardy!

The Serenity of Nature in Forgotten Places

In corners of streets where no one goes,
Nature giggles and brightly glows.
A rusty bicycle blooms wild and free,
As daisies peek out for you to see.

A lizard in sunglasses lounges with flair,
While dandelions drift without a care.
A raccoon hosts tea for the lost and stray,
With cookies made from yesterday's hay.

Forgotten benches dressed in ivy's kiss,
Invite the lonely to join in bliss.
A dreamer lies back, thoughts swirling around,
While nature whispers, "You're safe and sound."

So here in these spots, both silly and neat,
We savor the moments, we gather our seat.
In serenity's arms, we find our grace,
In forgotten places, our happy space.

Botanicals in a Concrete Sea

In a jungle of grey, I planted a shoe,
A daisy popped out, said, 'How do you do?'
Amongst hammers and nails, it waved with delight,
As a squirrel rolled by, it declared it a sight.

The fence offered advice, old and wise,
'Grow where you can, beneath gloomy skies.'
A cactus wore shades, took a sunbath at noon,
While the mailbox sang softly a very old tune.

Pigeons were judges, they fluffed up their tails,
As my fern tried to dance, but it tripped on the rails.
A clover in bloom, made a crown for my head,
As laughter erupted, from where the weeds spread.

So cheers to the plants, with their quirks and their flair,
In this pool of concrete, I'm crafting my lair.
Let's celebrate joy, in this odd little nook,
With a promise that someday, we'll write each a book.

Glimmers of Life in Ashen Corners

In corners where shadows once sat like a throne,
A potted brave cactus now claims the old zone.
It throws parties for roaches, spins tales of the floor,
While the light bulb above sighs, 'I need to explore!'

By the sink, sprigs of mint plot to take flight,
With whispers of cocktails to stir up the night.
They'll dance with the dishes till dawn starts to creep,
While vines climb the wall, trying not to peep.

A rubber plant giggles, says, 'All is well,'
Though the air's filled with tales from the dust and the smell.
Each pot holds a dream that escapes with a smile,
Turning stale moments into vintage style.

So here's to the quirks, painting colours in grey,
In this dim little room, come dance, come what may.
We'll spin into laughter, break boundaries in cheer,
As the blossoms remind us, adventure is near.

Verdure's Embrace in a Stark Space

In a box full of bricks, there's a leaf's daring dash,
Loudly calling the dust, 'Come join in the splash!'
A ficus did twirl, with its branches all wide,
While a shy little fern watched, with pins all applied.

'Chlorophyll vibes, let's have some fun,' said the jade,
As it plotted a coup against the carpet it played.
In a hushed little nook, where the whispers grew loud,
A dandelion chuckled, feeling like a cloud.

Sprouts forged a plan, to conquer the gloom,
With a tea party set among the cluttered room.
Cupcakes of soil and juice made from sun,
It turned into laughter, what's better than fun?

Here's to the plants, with their colorful glee,
They brighten my world, as they dance just for me.
In starkness they flourish, with stories to share,
Reminding us all to breathe deep, and care.

The Sigh of Leaves in Still Air

In a room built of silence, my spider plant sighed,
'We thrive in odd corners where chaos has tried.'
The candles all flickered, a party unsought,
While the ivy enviously plotted, and thought.

Coffee cups grinned with leftover routines,
As the chairs held debates of their past caffeine dreams.
Petunias spread gossip, while pears peeped with zest,
And the fridge joined the chatter, proud of its fest.

A celery dance broke out, twirling with flair,
'Cannot be contained, oh, life is a dare!'
In a world draped in stillness, they laughed and they played,
As the rug rolled its eyes, in delightful dismay.

So lift up your pots, and let giggles uncoil,
In the hush of this room, let the plants take the spoils.
For amidst all the grey, with their life so absurd,
They sprout joy in the silence—yes, haven't you heard?

Serenity Found in Forgotten Spaces

In a dusty room with a plant so small,
The cactus giggles, daring the wall.
While a chair sits comfy, with no one to share,
It dreams of a dance, but no one will care.

A sock left behind, hangs out with glee,
Recounting wild stories of socks that roam free.
The curtains sway gently, chasing a fly,
They plot a great escape, oh my, oh my!

An old lamp flickers, winks at the floor,
It keeps all the secrets of those who ignored.
In this quiet corner, hilarity blooms,
With laughter and whispers from inanimate rooms.

A lonely old book, covered in dust,
Whispers sweet nothings, in laughter we trust.
In forgotten spaces, joy we can find,
Where silliness thrives, and's always well-timed!

A Tapestry of Growth in Still Waters

A puddle reflects a duck's joyful quack,
While lilies play games, never looking back.
The reeds stand tall, like guards with a grin,
Whispering secrets to fish diving in.

An old boat rests, dreaming of sails,
Of grand ocean journeys and colorful tales.
But here on the bank, it's just taking naps,
Creating a laugh with its wonderful mishaps.

The dragonflies dance with a sprightly twist,
As frogs form a choir, they croak songs of bliss.
Amidst all this beauty, a snail takes its time,
Plotting a race that's silly and sublime.

From rocks to the reeds, where laughter is slow,
Nature's a jokester, with plenty to show.
In the still waters, excitement can rise,
As life spins a yarn, to no one's surprise!

The Allure of Life in Silence

In a quiet nook, the shadows do play,
Where dust bunnies giggle, come out to sway.
The clock ticks slowly, like a sleepy cat,
Waiting for mischief and a friendly spat.

The potted plant leans, stretching for sun,
Feigning sophistication, pretending it's fun.
While the curtains gossip and sway to a tune,
A calm atmosphere spun from a cartoon.

A squirrel outside plays hide and seek,
While the couch does sigh with a creaky squeak.
In silence, the fun spills into the air,
As laughter erupts from the corners laid bare.

In corners of stillness, joy hides its face,
Until a loud sneeze makes it spring from its place.
With all of these antics, life's simple delight,
Brings smiles in the quiet, morning to night!

Nature's Soliloquy in Quiet Quarters

The tree outside wears a crown made of leaves,
While grumpy old rocks chuckle in threes.
The sun peeks in, with a wink and a smile,
As shadows jive joyfully all the while.

An ant on a mission, with crumbs on a trek,
Turns, bumps a leaf, and falls like a wreck.
While grasshoppers tire from hopping all day,
Observing the mayhem—they just want to play.

In corners and nooks, the breeze shares its tale,
Of life in a whisper, or maybe a wail.
From petals to stones, humor twists and spins,
Nature's own jesters with quips on the winds.

With laughter erupting from pots and from cracks,
Life's funny moments all don mismatched slacks.
In quiet quarters, we find the best cheer,
As nature giggles, making mischief sincere!

Hiding Vibrance in Shadows

In corners dark, a gnome does peek,
With colorful bows and yellowed cheek.
He whispers jokes to a cat so sly,
While plants play poker, oh my, oh my!

A rogue fern twirls, a dance routine,
While dust bunnies giggle, oh so obscene.
A cactus crackles with puns to share,
As shadows giggle, unaware of their flair.

A lonely bulb flickers, feeling quite grand,
In a world where everything's quite bland.
The dragonfly's sipping on morning dew,
Comparing his wings—yellow to blue!

At nightfall, they plan a grand escape,
To paint the walls in colors, just gape!
But under the moon, it's back to the grind,
In shadows, vibrance is fun to find.

Stories Lurking Beneath the Surface

In the cracks of the wall, a tale is spun,
Of mismatched socks and the marathon run.
The radiator weeps over lost heat,
As roaches recount their last grand feat.

A puddle sways, it's got dreams of flight,
While the ceiling stains gossip by night.
Lamenting the jars left unopened black,
Oh, the stories they share behind our back!

A chair squeaks loud, it's seen it all,
The dance parties held in the dull-hued hall.
In whispers of dust, the past finds a way,
To giggle and chortle, come what may.

The rug holds secrets of shoes that tread,
On the path of laughter or tears that bled.
Together they plot, like a sitcom cast,
Reminding us all, dull times don't last.

Awaiting the Rebirth in a Dull Place

In the heart of a room where colors fell flat,
A sock puppet dreams of the grand aristocrat.
With plans for a pageant, it preens and it poses,
While the dust puffers simply dozes.

The wallpaper blushes in faint pastel hues,
As the frame holds a photo of yesterday's booze.
A spider weaves tales of webbing galore,
While the lamp dreads illuminating more.

Ah, the dream of a window, wide open, so bold,
With whispers of flowers, both young and old.
In a world made of frumps and forgotten spice,
They wait for the bloom, isn't that nice?

The drama's unfolding, a comedy grand,
As the rug lifts its fringe and takes a firm stand.
With every long sigh, they chortle again,
Awaiting the rebirth of joyful refrain.

Fresh Hope in Stagnant Air

In stagnant air, a tickle of zest,
A moth tries to tango, it believes it's the best.
With a flip and a flap, it twirls with glee,
Dreaming of breezes that set it free.

The old couch groans, it has tales to tell,
Of spilled snacks and laughter that rang like a bell.
A cushion shimmies with secrets and fun,
Waiting for a guest—a new friend to run.

Beneath the table, a potato sits tight,
Planning a journey to the sun, oh what a fright!
As dust motes dance like stars in the gloom,
Each one a wish for the bright to consume.

Yet in each still moment, a spark can ignite,
With giggles and grins that uplift the night.
So here's to the moments, both stale and unique,
Fresh hope is brewing, though it's a bit bleak.

Bitter-Sweet Leaves of Memory

In a pot full of dust, memories sprout,
Like weeds in a garden, they dance all about.
Coffee cups echo with laughter and sighs,
While socks disappear, oh, what a surprise!

The fridge hums a tune, out of time and place,
Leftovers whisper, 'Don't let us go to waste!'
The cat gives me side-eye, judging my style,
As if my bad dance moves could earn a guile.

Old photos are stuck to the walls like glue,
Reminding me gently of things that I knew.
Some dreams went stale, like bread in a bin,
Yet here I am laughing, where do I begin?

The clock ticks away, my humor runs dry,
But oh how I chuckle when life says 'Oh my!'
In the garden of memories, roots intertwine,
A bitter-sweet harvest, oh, how I define!

Flourishing Underneath the Surface

In a world where the dirt gets all the respect,
The plants have their secrets, it takes a sharp intellect.
Sneaky little daisies, with petals so bright,
Hide in the shadows, just out of the light.

Beneath the old concrete, the grass makes its play,
While pigeons just sit there, judging all day.
Who's really winning in this game of the fittest?
Is it our pet cactus, or just a bit of wistness?

I talk to my flowers, they nod and they sway,
While my neighbor's lawn glares, 'Why don't you just pay?'
But in my funny jungle, the humor's my shield,
As blossom-filled battles bring joy to the field.

Through cracks in the pavement, sprouts giggle and mock,
Each bloom a reminder – I'm never a rock.
So call me eccentric, I'll wear it with pride,
In this riot of color, I've got nothing to hide!

Beyond the Gloom of Yesterday

Yesterday's blues can pack quite a punch,
But here comes today with a feisty crunch.
With socks that don't match, and hair full of bed,
I step into sunlight, and dance on my head.

The clouds throw a fit, like they're drawn on a board,
While I spin in circles, oh my, I'm adored.
My neighbors peek out, with eyes full of awe,
At my groovy moves, amidst yesterday's flaw.

Who knew that a bun could double as art?
Or that a watermelon could play a key part?
With laughter as loud as a trumpet parade,
I'll embrace all the mess, and let worries fade.

Beyond Gloomy Jim and his frown of the year,
Are colorful dreams that I hold oh so dear.
In the theater of life, I'm a clumsy old star,
Shining amidst shadows, hoorah, here we are!

A World Awash in Subtle Hues

In a spectrum of chaos, colors collide,
While my cat on the couch delivers his pride.
Once we laughed at the furniture's great fate,
Now it's their turn to laugh at our state.

Each spill tells a story, a mural of life,
From coffee to crumbs, oh the tales rife with strife.
The curtains hang dusty, draped like an old shroud,
They whisper to secrets as I act out loud.

Throw my socks in a pile, make a rainbow of mess,
The laundry's a puzzle, how can I distress?
My plants, they keep laughing, with leaves all a-twirl,
As I flail in such splendor, they nod at the whirl.

So here in this place, with all its bright flaws,
I embrace the absurd, just because I can pause.
In a world full of colors, let's dance in the hue,
With laughter the pigment, each day feels brand new!

www.ingramcontent.com/pod-product-compliance
Lightning Source LLC
Chambersburg PA
CBHW070303120526
44590CB00017B/2548